Forget For Success

Walking Away from Outdated, Counterproductive Beliefs and People Practices

Things To Forget Today

- People should be treated equally.
- Different = Wrong
- Diversity is a numbers game
- What you don't know won't hurt you

Eric Harvey and Steve Ventura

a *WALK THE TALK®* handbook

To order additional copies of *Forget For Success,*
or for information on other
WALK THE TALK® products and services,
please contact us at **800.888.2811**
or visit our website at
www.walkthetalk.com

Values Based Business Solutions

©1997 by Performance Systems Corporation. All rights reserved. No part of this book may be reproduced in any form without written permission from the publisher.

Published by: Performance Publishing Company, a subsidiary of
                 Performance Systems Corporation
                 2925 LBJ Freeway, Suite 201
                 Dallas, Texas 75234-7614
                 972.243.8863

Performance Publishing books may be purchased for educational, business, or sales promotional use.

WALK THE TALK® is a registered trademark of Performance Systems Corporation.

Book design by Joseph Rattan Design
Cover photograph by Rusty Hill Photogrpahy

Printed in the United States of America.
10 9 8 7 6 5 4 3 2

ISBN: 1 - 885228 - 29 - 5

NOT To Be Forgotten

*V*ery special thanks ...
to our friend and teammate

Juli Baldwin

for her superior "behind the scenes" work
in helping successfully turn our ideas
into books, and to our colleagues and clients

Brian Clark
Bob Coulter
Jean Gilroy
Al Lucia
Joel Marks
Karl Schoemer

for their invaluable contributions to this work.

My experiences have shown me that life truly is a journey, and the less baggage we carry the easier the ride.

Wally Amos
Founder, Famous Amos Cookies

So much to *remember,* so little *storage space.*

*E*ver get headaches from seemingly endless lists of things to remember in order to be successful? *We* sure do! And we really don't care much about studies that prove humans use only a small percentage of their total brain capacity. We still experience the all too common phenomenon known as "information overload."

It's like the sky is filled with bombers loaded with rules, procedures, models, protocols, techniques, buzzwords, habits, strategies, keys, secrets ... and your head is ground zero. And, of course, every new book you pick up just adds to the "remember this" load.

Well, this book is different. This book will ease your burden by identifying many beliefs, ideas, old adages, and traditional business lore that you can forget. Yes, we did say FORGET!

The fact is, we all carry a certain amount of counterproductive cerebral baggage that weighs us down ... and holds us back.

Our loads include everything from once valid beliefs and practices that have outlived their usefulness and applicability – to misinformation and misconceptions that we've accepted (and even embraced) without much examination or thought.

Why care about this "baggage"? Because it negatively impacts us, the people we work with, the environment we work in, and the results we get. Simply stated, whatever we accept and believe determines how we behave … and how we behave determines what we achieve (or don't achieve). Regardless of our good intentions, we're all susceptible to flawed thinking that eventually leads to flawed end states. But dump this data from our memory banks, and we free up space for more productive alternatives – we make room for the good stuff … "the right stuff."

So read on. Accept the challenge of walking away from beliefs and resulting behaviors that do not serve you or your organization well. Accept the challenge to …

FORGET FOR SUCCESS.

people should be treated equally

*R*emember this whenever **all** people and **all** situations are **exactly** the same (as in never). Otherwise ... FORGET IT!

Here we have a good intention gone awry. To treat people equally is to assume that everyone comes to the party with the same skills, backgrounds, biases, motivations, knowledge, abilities, and performance records. It presupposes that all contributions and circumstances are identical. We all know that's rarely the case.

Let's say two colleagues are late for work on the same day. One – with a great attendance record – needed to arrange for a sick child. The other has a lousy record and once again just couldn't seem to make it in on time. Should they be treated exactly the same? Or, how about two kids that get straight B's on their report cards. One really didn't work that hard at it, while the other busted their rear to make the grade. Should they be treated equally? What do you think? We think NOT!

> *Rather than treating people equally, your focus should be on treating them equitably.*

Check the dictionary – there is a difference. *Equal* means "the same; identical." *Equitable* means "reasonable; just." So, when you treat people equitably, you treat them the way they deserve to be treated ... based on the specific facts and circumstances at hand. There's a term for that. It's called **fairness**.

> *People aren't the same all over.*

recognition is the same as reward

*F*orget it! Ever heard someone say: "I don't believe in rewarding people for just doing what they're supposed to do"? Maybe you've said it (or thought it) yourself. Well, we agree with that phrase. Rewards are special things that should be reserved for special times. Too often, however, people incorrectly equate recognition with reward. As a result, it isn't given as often as it could be or should be.

The root of recognition is the word *recognize* which means "to acknowledge; to take notice of; to appreciate." So when people "just do what they're supposed to do," is that worthy of an acknowledgement? Should it be noticed? Should it be appreciated? We sure as heck hope so!

Do you receive enough acknowledgement and appreciation for the good, solid work that you do? Most people don't think so ... and that probably includes a bunch of the folks that work with and for you. Eliminate any thoughts that recognition is the same as reward, and you just might be more inclined to ...

> *frequently notice and reinforce the kind of behavior and performance you want from others*

... and you'll still have rewards available for the really super stuff.

To be sure, the type and amount of recognition should vary according to the situation and individual involved. And if you want to find out *how* people would like to be recognized, ask them!

> *A little recognition goes a long way – and it's a darned good thing.*

apply your best resources to your worst performing areas

aka: Sic your stronger performers on your weaker operations

At first glance this seems natural and very appropriate. But if you're inclined to follow it as standard operating procedure, our best advice is to give it a second thought ... and then FORGET IT!

> *In the long run, you'll be much better off using your best resources in areas of strength rather than problem zones.*

There's a classic question in the sales and marketing area that helps make our point: Should you put your best salesperson in your worst territory or your best territory? The traditional "management by exception" perspective (i.e., focus on what's *not* working) would suggest that the best salesperson should go to the worst area and fix it. Indeed, that seems flawlessly logical. But what if we add the following to the scenario: 1) the worst territory is currently producing $10,000 per month; 2) the best territory is producing $100,000 per month; and 3) the best salesperson can double sales in his or her area. What seems logical now? Where's the biggest bang for the buck (highest ROI)?

Don't misunderstand – we're not suggesting you ignore your weak zones. Just make sure you don't concentrate so heavily on fixing what you're doing wrong that you neglect to expand and capitalize on what you're doing right ... and squander your best people and physical resources in the process.

> *Sez our Aussie colleague Brian Clark: If you only work on your weaknesses, you just might end up with a business filled with very strong weaknesses!*

It isn't so astonishing,
>   the number of things
I can remember,
>   as the number of things
I can remember
>   that aren't so.

>   *Mark Twain*

Three Ways To Order
Forget For Success

Call: 800.888.2811
Fax: 972.243.0815
Mail: The WALK THE TALK® Company
2925 LBJ Freeway, Suite 201
Dallas, Texas 75234-7614

(see order form on back)

Ask about our other high-impact publications:

- *Walk The Talk ... And Get The Results You Want*

  The best-selling business book that shows leaders, at all levels, why and how to turn organizational values into value-added practices.

- *144 Ways To Walk The Talk*

  The quick-reference handbook packed with proven ideas and strategies for practicing values-driven leadership.

- *Walking The Talk Together: An Employee Handbook*

  The powerful handbook that encourages all employees to take responsibility for values-driven business practices.

- *Walk Awhile In MY Shoes*

  The revolutionary *2-in-1* handbook that encourages understanding, empathy, and cooperation between managers and employees.

For information on these and other WALK THE TALK® products and services, call us at 800.888.2811 or visit our website at **www.walkthetalk.com**

Values **B**ased **B**usiness **S**olutions

The WALK THE TALK® Company
2925 LBJ Freeway, Suite 201, Dallas, Texas 75234-7614
972.243.8863 • Fax 972.243.0815 • www.walkthetalk.com

Forget For Success
Order Form

82LL

Copies	
1-99 – $6.95 each	
100-999 – $6.45 each	
1000-4999 – $5.95 each	
5000-9999 – $5.45 each	
10,000 or more – $4.95 each	

Book Total $_____

Shipping and Handling *(see chart below)* +$_____

TOTAL $_____

Texas Only – Sales Tax (8.25% of Total) +$_____

TEXAS TOTAL $_____

SHIPPING & HANDLING CHARGES:

Order $ Amount	Charges
Up to $50	$4
$50-99	$7
$100-249	$10
$250-649	$18
$650-1,299	$32
$1,300-1,999	$55
$2,000-3,499	$68
Over $3,500	Call

Outside the continental U.S., please call.

Orders shipped via UPS Ground. Next business day and second business day delivery is available. Please call for information.

☐ **YES**, please send me information on other WALK THE TALK® products and services to help turn organizational values into value-added results.

Name (MR/MS) _____

Title _____

Organization _____

Street Address _____

City, State, Zip, Country _____

Phone ( ) _____ Fax ( ) _____

Purchase Order Number (if applicable) _____

☐ MasterCard ☐ VISA ☐ American Express Cards ☐ Check Enclosed ☐ Please Invoice
(Payable to: The WALK THE TALK Company) (orders over $100 only)

Account Number _____ Exp. _____

Signature _____

Prices effective November 1997 are subject to change. Orders payable in U.S. dollars. Orders outside U.S. and Canada must be prepaid.

different = wrong

Sometimes yes, sometimes no. But accept this as an absolute, and you have the basis for polarization, prejudice, and lunkhead thinking. FORGET IT! We repeat, FORGET IT!

Generalizing that different is wrong stems from the belief that our way is the only right way. Example: "People in many foreign countries drive on the wrong side of the road!" In our country that may be true, but in their homelands, their driving behaviors are correct. What's factual in this example is that they drive on a *different* side of the road. Their way would be wrong only if they were driving here and operating their vehicles contrary to our traffic laws. And of course, our way would be wrong if we drove in their country.

The real danger with the "different equals wrong" perspective comes when it is applied to people. There aren't enough pages in this book to cover the volume of problems inherent to such short-sighted thinking. We couldn't possibly do justice to the subject – so we won't try. We merely offer this to ponder: No two people on this earth are exactly alike – we're all unique, we're all different. So, if different is wrong, WE'RE ALL WRONG! Megabummer!

Forget any thoughts that different is inherently wrong and you'll be more receptive to fresh ideas, creative people, and positive change. Take this to the bank:

> *With few exceptions, different isn't wrong ...*
> *it's just different.*

You see, it's difference that brings us invention, innovation, variety, and choice. It's difference that gives us our heroes. And, it's difference that makes the people we care about "special."

My kids are all very different. I wonder which one is right?

10 Phrases to FORGET That Stifle Creativity and Initiative

1. "We've tried that before"

So what? Just because something didn't work in the past doesn't mean it won't work now ... especially if you try a different spin, or just do it better. You shouldn't ignore past experiences, but you don't want to be hampered by them, either.

2. "That'll never work"

Unless you're so sure that you'd bet your life on it, forget this one. It's way too easy to get sucked into the Self-Fulfilling Prophecy: If you expect something to fail from the start, you'll unconsciously act in ways that make failure more likely to occur. It's a fact!

3. "They'll never let us do that"

(See #2 above. Same trap, same response.)

4. "Yes, but ... "

Want to know the fastest way to render the word "yes" meaningless? Follow it with "but." In most cases, you might as well just say "no"! Once you forget this word combo, you'll be more open to using an inspiring "Yes, and ... ," which helps maintain a positive focus.

5. "I already know how it will turn out"

It must be nice to have such a handle on the future. Unfortunately, the crystal ball in *our* office has a crack in it (otherwise, we'd spend a lot more on lottery tickets). The fact is, you only THINK you know ... and you've got as much chance of being wrong as you do of being right.

6. "That's not how I would do it"

Yeah, so? And your way may not be how others would do things, either. Again, so? As long as the results are there, everyone needs a little freedom to do things their way. Besides, "their way" just might end up being a *better* way. Imagine that!

7. "We've always done it that way"

Another so what! Here's a lesson from Reality 101: If you keep on doing what you've always done, you'll keep on getting what you've always got. Granted, "what you've always got" may be pretty darn good. But maintaining the status quo offers little opportunity for improvement.

8. "Nobody else does it that way"

Maybe, maybe not. Maybe there's a good reason, or maybe nobody else has thought of it yet. One thing's for sure – every invention and innovation that's ever been developed was, at one time, a deviation from the way everybody else did it.

9. "We've got more than enough good ideas"

If that's the case, how about shipping a few to the rest of us who are struggling to come up with more. If you're lucky enough to work with people who are always thinking, dreaming, and exploring possibilities, count your blessings. And whatever you do, don't discourage them. They're your future!

10. "Whose idea was this, anyway?"

Forget the *who*, remember the *what*. Focus on the merits of the idea rather than on the source. The *who* part is only important when you need to track down the source for more clarity … or to offer recognition.

Brains are like closets. Over time, they become filled with things we no longer use – things that no longer fit. Every once in a while they need to be cleaned out!

people need to be managed

*W*rong again! FORGET IT! Processes need to be managed, money needs to be managed, priorities need to be managed, and so on. But people need to be *led* (as in that "leadership" stuff that leaders do).

Look up the word *manage* in any dictionary or basic business text and you find the same general definition: "to administer; to control." Look up *lead* and you find a very different meaning: "to show the way; to inspire." Compare these sets of definitions. Which seems more appropriate for building a climate of commitment and productivity? Which is more likely to bring out the very best in people? Which approach do *you* respond best to – being managed or being led?

> *Forget any thoughts about managing people, and you'll free up the brain space necessary to focus on leading them.*

Need some clues on how to be a good leader? Start by completing the following sentence: "I do my best and most effective work for leaders who … " Once you've identified the characteristics and behaviors of leaders who inspire you, follow their lead.

So, what do you do if you encounter one of those very rare problem people who just won't respond to good leadership? Fight the tendency to try to control them. Just show them the way – or the way *out*!

Not all leaders are bosses … and not all bosses are leaders.

as long as you don't hear from me, you'll know you're doing okay

aka: No news is good news; Silence is golden

Yeah, right, uh huh. FORGET IT!

This is a case of a good intention being camouflaged with nonsense. The hidden good intention: "Do your job well, and I won't bug you." The nonsense: "By me saying nothing, you'll know exactly what I'm thinking and feeling." Unless the people you work with are clairvoyant, you can flush this one away.

> The only time people really know what you're thinking is when you <u>tell</u> them. Short of that, they're left trying to figure out what's on your mind.

Can you think of a time when you had a problem with someone, but – because you were busy, or angry, or uncomfortable addressing the issue – you said nothing? Ever had someone a little steamed at you but you didn't know about it for some time? Of course. The fact is that silence is not approval, and it's not golden ... it's just silence.

Purge this one from your cerebral cortex, and you'll make room for better, more productive ideas ... like bothering *with* folks when they do good work, and when they don't – like letting folks regularly hear from you. That's *feedback*. And far too often, that's rare!

> *If you ignore other people, does that make you an ignor-amus?*

values are important to know

*C*lose, but no cigar! Place too much emphasis on knowing your organization's values backwards and forwards, and you'll miss *their* point ... and *the* boat. When it comes to mere knowledge or lip service, FORGET IT!

Before reading on, write your answers to the following:

What is the purpose of organizational values? Why do they exist?

_____
_____
_____
_____
_____

Now, look at what you wrote. Did you say that values exist just to give people something to know and talk about? We bet not! Chances are you concluded that values exist to provide direction ... to guide individual and group actions and decisions. Correctamundo! And the key word there is "actions."

Forget just knowing about your organizational values, and you'll be more likely to ...

> *focus on what's truly important: <u>behaving</u> those values ... focus on walking the talk.*

What specifically are you and others doing to bring your values and good intentions to life? *That's* what you really need to know!

> *In the end, do you suppose St. Peter will care much about what we KNEW?*

The best way to break a bad habit is to drop it!

Unknown

treat people the way you want to be treated

*N*ope. FORGET IT!

Now, if you think we've gone too far by defaming the Golden Rule, take a deep breath and chill out. That's not what this is about. We don't challenge the spirit or wisdom of that ageless classic one bit. We do, however, believe that its literal application can be problematic.

To think that people want to be treated just like us is to assume that people *are* just like us. And that just isn't so. Sure, we all have many things in common. But we also have distinct differences — needs, interests, fears, desires, lifestyles, challenges, and dreams — that make us unique.

> *One surefire way to succeed in business and life is to treat people the way they want to be treated.*

That's been called the Platinum Rule, and it requires people to know something about the other people they interact with. All of us need to find out what makes others tick — what "floats their boats "— and use that information in our dealings with them. It all starts by asking folks what's important to them.

Forget about treating people like *you* want to be treated and you'll be more open to dealing with them as the unique individuals they are.

Do you suppose the Marquis de Sade practiced the Golden Rule?

make the punishment fit the crime

aka: People who screw up should be punished

Unless you're dealing with a hard-core criminal, put a stick of dynamite next to this one and light the fuse! FORGET IT!

This carryover from the criminal justice system (and Victorian child rearing) just doesn't cut it at work – especially in today's competitive business environment where your goal must be to build commitment and individual responsibility. Punishment will get you neither. It's not a corrective strategy. More often than not, it's just an emotional response … and a counterproductive one at that.

With few exceptions, people don't respond progressively better when they are treated progressively worse. They respond in kind (you know, what goes around comes around). They frequently engage in "get by" or "get even" behaviors, learn merely to avoid getting caught, or take the hit and consider the score even. But no matter what they do, they'll undoubtedly conclude they owe you zilch when it comes to commitment, productivity, and responsible adult behavior.

Abandon the punishment mindset and you'll be able to more clearly …

focus on problem-solving strategies.

When you handle them right, the vast majority of people will respond properly. So, what about the small percentage that don't? They should be given the opportunity to work for a competitor. That's not punishment, that's separation!

If punishment really works, why do we have "repeat offenders"?

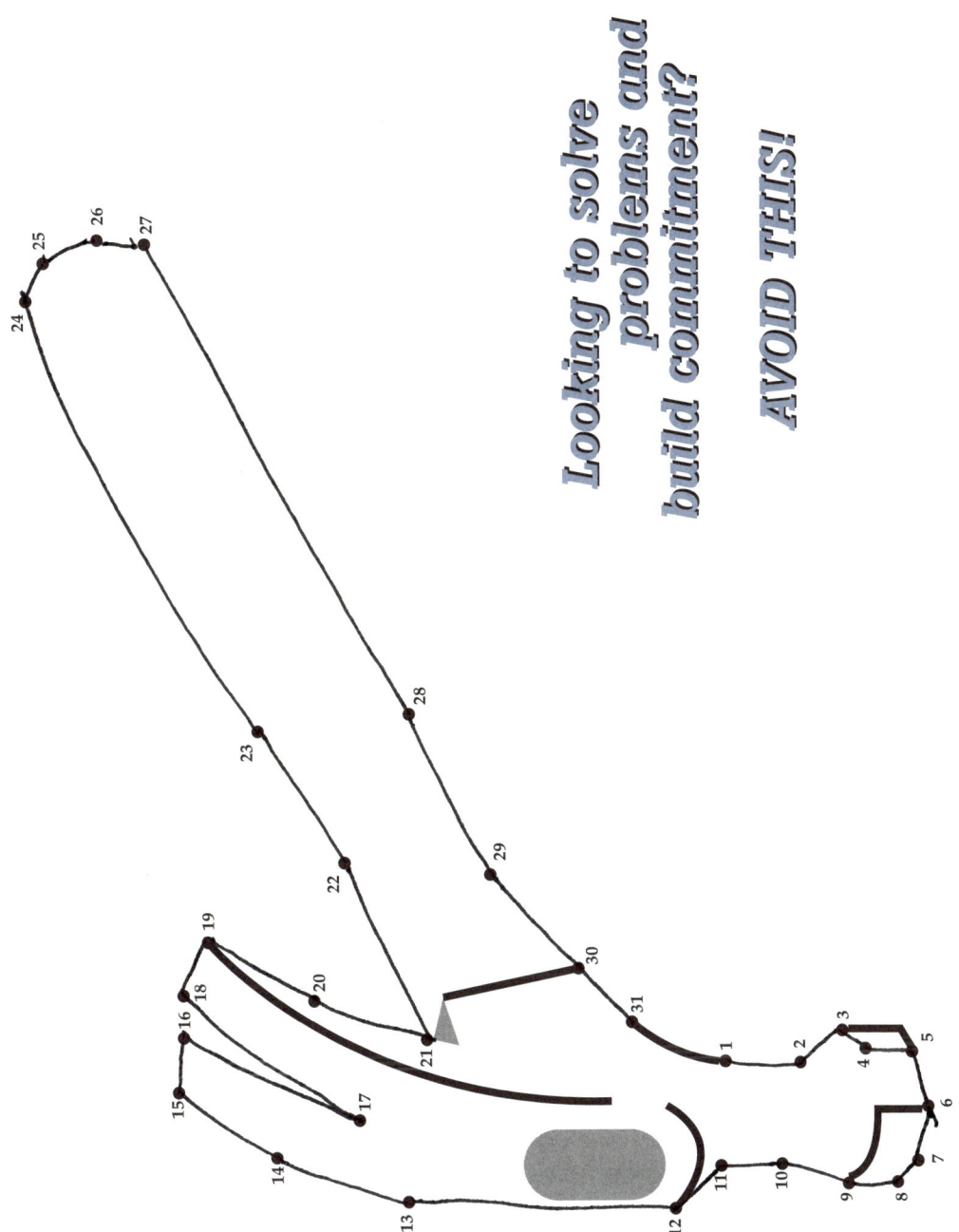

diversity is really a numbers game

*H*ave "a friend" who thinks this? Tell them to wake up and smell the new millennium! Diversity isn't about numbers, and it's not a game. So, FORGET IT … twice!

If there was a list of the most misconceived and misunderstood topics in business today, **diversity** would no doubt be right at the top. For many, it's an emotional issue – often stained with the residue of negative past experiences and well-intended but ineffective "programs." Some see it as a way to correct past injustices. Others link it with the words "quota" and "affirmative action." Well, we'd like to set the record straight – at least as we see it. Diversity isn't about numbers, games, quotas, or social injustice. Diversity is about competitive advantage … it's about GOOD BUSINESS.

Organizations that build and embrace diverse workforces tend to be better at understanding and responding to (i.e. capturing larger shares of) today's ever-changing global and local marketplaces. They're more likely to be viewed as "employers of choice" – allowing them to recruit and retain the very best people. And they enjoy exposure to a wider range of ideas and perspectives, which leads to new and improved products and services. That's great stuff that many competitors would kill for.

Forget the "numbers game," and it's more likely you'll …

> *see diversity for what it really is: a business success strategy*

… one that can improve organizational performance and ultimately protect a lot of jobs – including yours.

> *Want to be successful in business? Diversify!*

what you don't know can't hurt you

aka: Ignorance is bliss

*F*orget this one real fast!

What you don't know not only *can* hurt you, it can also put a serious dent in your career. Stuff is happening all around you at warp speed. Fail to keep up with technology advances, new work procedures, changes in your industry, changes in your company, refinements in people skills, and the like, and you might find yourself passed over … and passed by. If you're a "short timer," counting the days to retirement, you may not care. But if you're planning on being around for awhile, it would be wise to examine the priorities you've placed on personal development, continuous learning, and just plain knowing what's going on around you.

Occasionally, we all face the temptation to rest on our laurels – you know, when you think, "I'm done with school, I know my job, I'm good at what I do, and all I have to do is come to work, perform, and go home." Beware! There's a false sense of security hissing there that eventually will bite you.

Forget the notion that what you don't know can't hurt you, and you'll be more apt to …

> *look for and create opportunities to learn, grow, and continually improve.*

Where is your organization headed? Where is your industry headed? Do you have the information, knowledge, and skills necessary to be part of the future … or are *you* headed for Jurassic Park?

People who think ignorance is bliss probably are very blissful.

definition of a good employee: someone who works hard

Sorry, but as the old song title goes, *It Ain't Necessarily So.* FORGET IT!

In today's fast-paced, competitive, and often resource-depleted business arena …

> *a good employee is someone who adds value and gets results*

… someone who is productive and makes a positive difference. We appreciate hard workers as much as anyone. But working hard and getting results aren't necessarily the same.

Test this yourself. Let's say your car developed a problem, so you took it to the shop. It's been two days, and now you've come to pick it up. Imagine if, after handing you a big fat bill, the mechanic said, "I didn't fix your car, but I worked really hard." You'd probably be more than a little torqued (mechanic pun!). Of course you expected the mechanic to work hard – that's a given. What you were paying the mechanic for, however, was to solve your problem … to make a positive difference. He didn't, so he failed – regardless of his work ethic.

Forget hard work as the primary criterion for evaluating yourself and others, and you'll find it easier to focus on what truly makes a "good" employee good: **value-added results.**

To make a positive difference or not to make a positive difference? *That* is the question.

> *What good is double time if you're running in the wrong direction?*

More Phrases ... to FORGET

A lighthearted look

Forget ...	*If you're really thinking ...*
1. "That's interesting"	"Yuck!"
2. "It needs just a little more work"	"This dog needs a total overhaul"
3. "Whenever you get a chance"	"I want it yesterday"
4. "I've never seen it done quite like that before"	"I hope I never see it done like that again"
5. "Let me give that some thought"	"I'll wait a while before I say no"
6. "Let me know if I can help"	"You're on your own, Charlie"
7. "That's different"	"Double yuck!"

Okay, we admit it. This page is intended to make you laugh. But it's also intended to make the point that all of us say things we really don't mean. Sometimes, in an effort to be considerate and tactful, we're less than honest. And that can be a problem since others tend to take our words literally – they assume we mean what we say, and they act accordingly.

Here are two things NOT to forget: 1) honesty really *is* the best policy, and 2) you can be honest without being brutal. Saying "I have some problems with that" is obviously much better than "yuck" ... and a lot more honest than "that's interesting."

FORGET quality comes from "the Quality Program"

*N*ope. FORGET IT!

To be sure, quality programs and processes are good, important, and needed. They provide standards, strategies, and measurements that are vital for continuous-improvement efforts. But processes are not panaceas. Put all your attention and effort on "the system," and you'll overlook a simple, real-world fact:

> *Quality comes from a quality culture ... quality comes from people. It happens one day at a time, one person at a time, one behavior at a time.*

No great revelation here, you say. It's obvious that people are the key. Well, it's not always so apparent when you look at how organizations behave. Too many have fallen into the trap of building a detailed system, admiring it from afar, activating it, and then sitting back waiting for something to happen. The result? Zip! Nada! Nothing!

Lose the misconception that quality comes primarily from quality programs, and you'll free yourself to focus on people practices such as selection, training, coaching, feedback, recognition, etc. They're the best "quality programs" of all.

Besides, it's not the management of quality that matters most ... it's the quality of management!

> *What if your Quality Program showed up for work, but your people didn't?*

if people are having too much fun, they can't be working

aka: If people are laughing or staring into space, they must be goofing off

Can you say HOGWASH boys and girls? The key words here are "can't be" and "must be." Certainly, not everyone who laughs or stares into space is working. But to believe that they *can't* be working if they engage in those behaviors is just plain wrong. FORGET IT!

Each year, organizations around the world spend hundreds of thousands to millions of dollars on change and improvement strategies. Among the many areas of common focus are bringing enjoyment to the workplace (often characterized by laughter) and fostering creativity (sometimes characterized by staring into space – as in thinking!). Why all the money and time spent on those initiatives? Because they foster positive and creative corporate cultures that energize people and improve the bottom line. And yet, sometimes our first and most natural reaction is to be suspicious when we see the very behaviors those strategies are designed to produce.

Forget this misconception, and you'll be more likely to …

> encourage enjoyment and thinking. Be grateful when you see them … and be concerned when you don't.

> First, they wanna laugh. Then, they wanna think. The next thing you know, they'll wanna increase productivity. Whatever happened to the good old days?

I bear no grudges.
I have a mind that
retains nothing.

Bette Midler

all we need are a few big changes

*H*ow about one big FORGET IT!

No doubt most of us, at one time or another, have felt that our organizations were in desperate need of some reeeeally big changes – you know, the kind that cure all our ills in one fell swoop. And you may feel that same need sometime in the future. Our best advice: Don't sit on the sidelines holding your breath! If you're looking for true changes that last, you need to focus on lots of little things done over and over by lots of people ... including you.

Take a look at what separates winning people and companies from the "also rans." Compare those who walk the talk and those who don't. The winners aren't unique because of one or two gigantic things they do one hundred percent better than the rest of the field. Rather, they're profoundly different because of the hundreds of things they do ten percent better. No quick fixes, instant solutions, or "programs of the year" for these folks. They work hard at managing "the small stuff"; they understand that you can't do big stuff every day.

Are we saying that large, complex change strategies are never appropriate? Not on your life! We're merely suggesting that in the long run you'll be better off if you ...

> *devote more of your time, attention, and focus to doing a lot of little things a little bit better.*

That's real. That's doable. That's change.

Over time, small change can add up to big bucks.

"How About ... " and "Don't Think So" Sound Bites

Continually look for what's wrong and fix it

How about *every once in a while, look for what's **right** and celebrate it!* Sure, life is filled with lots of failures and frustrations, making it all too easy to focus on the negative. But life brings plenty of joys and successes, too. It's our choice whether we scorn the rain or celebrate the sunrise. One thing's for sure, however, the more successes we celebrate, the more successes we get ... and the better we feel. You can take that to the bank.

She's a self-made woman/He's a self-made man

Don't think so! It's true that highly successful people have an above-average drive and commitment to achieve. But no one does it all by themselves – we're all supported by teachers, coaches, product and equipment makers, clothing and food providers, etc., etc., etc. So, what's the point here? It's simple: **Our success is dependent on other people.** Behaving like we know that is one of our many challenges.

Manage your time

How about *manage your **priorities!*** Time is a constant – it moves at its own 24-hours-per-day pace regardless of what we do. Priorities, on the other hand, are totally within our control. It's up to us to make sure we're appropriately dealing with the "truly important" rather than becoming a regular victim of the "always urgent."

Hearing = Listening

Don't think so! Most of us hear the same way, but we tend to listen very differently. And occasionally, we don't listen at all! Hearing is a mechanical process involving sound vibrations passing through the internal organs of the ear. Listening is an *interpretive* process – turning sound into meaning. To assume someone inherently listens because they can hear is like assuming someone can write merely because they can hold a pen. Not so! **Listening is a skill that must be developed.** It's an active process requiring energy, discipline, and lots of effort.

To be successful, you must have plans and goals

How about *to be successful, you must turn your plans and goals into **actions!*** How many times have you come across people who talk about their hopes, dreams, and lofty goals but never do anything to make them happen? These are well-intending folks who, as the old Texas expression goes, are "all hat and no cattle"! In the end, we'll all be judged not by what we dreamed or planned, but rather by what we did.

Efficiency = Effectiveness

Don't think so! Efficiency is doing things right … **effectiveness is doing *right* things right.** Adding one little word makes one great big difference. All of us, at one time or another, have fallen into the trap of doing a really good job on something that just didn't matter that much. The real trick is to be competent in tasks and activities that are important (i.e., offer a high return on our invested effort). Otherwise, we'll end up going broke – with little consolation in knowing we did it efficiently!

People are our most important assets

How about *people* (employees, customers, colleagues, and business partners) *are our **only** important assets!* Capital equipment can rust and break, products and services can turn tired and stale, and intellectual property can all too quickly lose its marketplace value. But energized employees, loyal customers, and committed and trusting colleagues and business partners will never lose their value or importance. They are the true wealth of every organization.

The customer is always right

Don't think so! Customers are human – prone to mistakes, misjudgments, inconsistencies, and occasional inconsiderate or irrational behaviors. And it's certainly not unusual to find customers who have no earthly idea what they want and/or need. Unfortunately, some people think it's okay to exercise and exhibit such imperfections simply because they're paying you money. Those folks and those behaviors just come with the customer service territory.

No, the customer isn't always right, but that really doesn't matter. **The customer *is* always the customer.** Right or wrong, they are the lifeblood of your business and they must be treated accordingly.

Listen and you will learn

How about ***teach** and you will learn!* Preparing to teach others can be an excellent way to sharpen your own knowledge and skills. Perhaps the nicest thing about teaching is that "students" aren't the only ones who learn and grow.

Everyone should want to be a leader

Don't think so! Some people truly are content with minimal levels of involvement, decision making, responsibility, and authority. And we shouldn't think less of them for it. In the real world, **some people are leaders and some are followers** … some folks are drivers and some are passengers. Not every job is for every person – and that includes the job of leader.

Decisions should be based on facts

How about *decisions should be based on facts* **and perceptions!** Don't misunderstand. We're not suggesting you make decisions so that people will *like* you. We do recommend, however, that you consider the anticipated (or existing) perceptions of customers, employees, the community, and other stakeholders as part of your decision-making process. You've heard it before: People's perceptions are their realities, and they do affect how others work with and for you … and whether or not they'll do business with you. Those *are* facts.

"Teams" are the universal answer

Don't think so! If they were, every organization would use them successfully. But look around you. Seems like for every team that's formed, two are disbanded. Why? Because team-based approaches aren't necessarily right for every task, every organization, or every culture. Formal, **structured teams should be a response to a need.** They should be formed only when there is a good reason to form them – and they should exist only as long as there's a good reason for them to exist. Otherwise, you have teams for teams' sake … and they can quickly become another "program of the year."

To be successful, people need more information

How about *to be successful, people need more **intelligence!*** No, we're not saying that people need more smarts (brain power). We're talking about collecting the right data, analyzing it properly, and deriving conclusions that can be used to better the business.

In today's high-tech cyberworld, most organizations can generate enough data and statistics to bury their workforces. The trick is to identify and disseminate useable data that helps people make better decisions. For example: Knowing how much of a product or service you sold last month may be nice and somewhat encouraging, but it won't necessarily help you do anything better next month. It's just data. Analyzing buyer profiles, on the other hand, tells you exactly *who* is buying. Knowing their level, function, industry, and how much they bought can help you target your product development, marketing, and sales efforts more effectively. That's *intelligence!*

In a participative environment, all decisions are group decisions

Don't think so! Yes, participative environments do provide greater opportunities for involvement in the decision-making process ... people at all levels are typically afforded more of a hand in daily operations than you'd find with traditionally managed workplaces. Businesses, however, aren't democracies. **While some decisions are made by committee vote, many aren't ... because they shouldn't be.** Some issues requiring decisions are personal or confidential. Some involve "big picture" considerations or high levels of accountability. Just like at home, sometimes the votes are counted, sometimes they're "weighed," and sometimes they're not taken at all.

Old people aren't forgetful. They've just learned that most things aren't worth remembering.

Gary Apple
Humorist

formal performance appraisals are the best source of developmental feedback

Oh, if it were only true! FORGET IT! We plan to write a very short book entitled, *People Who Are Completely Satisfied With Their Performance Appraisal Process* – just as soon as we find enough folks to write about. We've been looking for over twenty-two years now.

Our experiences tell us that most formal performance appraisal processes are less than effective as sources of **developmental** feedback. Why? Two reasons. First, they're usually clouded with other agendas like salary administration, employee ranking, etc. It's awfully hard to concentrate on personal development while you're waiting to find out how much money you'll get (or won't get), or where you fall in the overall pecking order. Second, appraisals usually come from a single source – the boss. That makes them far too easy to reject with rationales such as "She/he's not around me enough to know what I really do" or "He/she's got it in for me" or "How can my boss evaluate me when she/he can't even do my job?" In the end, the feedback is discounted … and not used.

If you're looking to help others (and yourself) grow and improve, forget relying solely on formal systems.

The best feedback is frequent, developmentally oriented, and comes from multiple sources.

It's up to you to make it happen. Regularly let people know how they're doing. Discuss strengths as well as opportunities for improvement. Encourage them to ask others for feedback … and make sure *you* do the same.

Waiting for a formal system to ensure effective communication and feedback? Get a good book and a comfortable chair. It'll be a while.

supervisors are responsible for employee behavior

*I*t's time to erase the tape on this traditional and very parental mindset. Let it go … FORGET IT!

Everyone knows (at least intellectually) that adulthood equates to responsibility. Once people reach a certain age – usually eighteen – they're accountable for themselves. Whether or not they act like adults is irrelevant – they still own their behavior. Too often, however, these same adults go to work and perform under supervisors who behave the belief that *they* are responsible for the actions and behaviors of their reports. Well, it doesn't take a quantum physicist to figure out that if the boss takes the responsibility, the employees don't have it anymore. If you do all the thinking for others, make all the decisions for them, solve all their problems, correct their errors, and fail to hold them accountable, they become **non**-responsible … and act accordingly. Alas, a monster of your own creation.

Forget any notions that you're responsible for others, or that others are responsible for you, and you'll be primed to accept reality:

Everyone is responsible for their own behavior.

To be sure, supervisors must lead, coach, and deal with occasional employee performance problems. But in doing so, they've got to avoid making the employees' decisions for them. It's the difference between saying, "There's a problem. Here's what *I* want you to do … " and "There's a problem. What are *you* going to do?"

I do everything for them, and they still act like children … I don't get it.

empathy is a touchy-feely thing for wimps

*T*his is Cro-Magnon thinking. FORGET IT!

> *To be empathetic is to be understanding and considerate ... to attempt to see things from another person's perspective.*

It's walking awhile in someone else's shoes – there's nothing "touchy-feely" about it. We all want and need empathy. And we all get frustrated and discouraged when others fail to give it to us.

Empathy stems from the acceptance of four facts of life: 1) there are other people in this world besides me; 2) there are other viewpoints in this world besides mine; 3) your feelings and beliefs are just as important and valid to you as mine are to me; and 4) the better we understand each other, the better we'll be able to work together and contribute to each other's success.

Empathetic people realize that you don't have to agree with different perspectives in order to understand and accept them. They make a genuine effort to uncover all sides of an issue before acting or judging. And they look for opportunities to cut others the same slack they want for themselves.

So, forget any sensitivity training, T-group, "Let's all sit in a circle and sing 'Kumbaya'" notions you've ever had or heard about empathy. We're talking understanding here. We're talking being considerate. We're talking humanity.

> *Empathy, schmempathy! The real problem is no one understands what I go through.*

some rules are meant to be broken

*W*hich rules would those be? Certainly not any that *you* make at work (or around your house), right? Right! FORGET IT!

> *Rules are meant to be followed. If they weren't, they'd be called "suggestions."*

Most of us know that intellectually. We just don't always *behave* like we know it ... or like we believe it. To make the point, we once again turn to traffic laws. Who among us can honestly say they follow **all** the rules of the road **all** the time? (If you raised your hand, your application for sainthood will arrive soon by mail.) Most of our driving violations are unconscious and unintentional. Some, however, are very conscious and very intentional. And we often rationalize and excuse them with phrases such as: "I obey the important ones" or "It's okay because I did it safely" or "I was running late today." Multiply this behavior by the number of people on the road – each person complying with only those rules that he or she thinks are important – and you end up with mass chaos and a bunch of wrecks.

The same is true at work. Ignore or bend a rule, and you make it okay for others to do the same. Eventually, everyone chooses which regulations they'll follow and which ones they'll ignore. Then you have big problems.

But what should you do if you come across a rule that no longer serves your organization or your customers? Make it your personal mission to get it changed. If it really is a "bad" rule, there ought to be plenty of evidence to make your case.

> *Life would be a lot easier if they'd just put a special code on those rules that are okay to ignore.*

got a problem? take it to the boss

A heartfelt FORGET IT message from bosses everywhere:

"Thanks a lot, pal! Hope you feel better whenever you lighten your load by adding to mine. Like you, I'm dealing with a bunch of responsibilities, too little time, too many competing priorities, too few resources, a ton of change, and one or two charm-and-cooperation school dropouts. Imagine my pure joy at the chance of getting even more challenges to overfill my day.

"Whew! Now I feel better! With that woe-is-me out of the way, let me offer some less emotional clarity to this issue. Yes, we do have an 'open door policy' here. And yes, we (management) really mean it when we say we want to know about your concerns, issues, and problems. I sure would appreciate it, however, if you'd take a stab at solving problems – or at least identifying possible solutions – *before* you come to me. That way we'll start off in a problem-**solving** mode rather than a problem-**celebrating** mode.

"Think about the issue and its impact on you and others. Identify a few alternative solutions – weighing the pros and cons of each. And, be prepared to discuss what you've already done to try to resolve the issue. I'll usually be willing to devote as much time, attention, and effort to your problems as you."

Got a problem or complaint?

Take it to your brain before you take it to your boss.

Problem solving and positive change have something in common – they both begin with ME. And each of us is ME!

people today have a poor work ethic

A gut-level FORGET IT message from individual people today:

"Well, pal, you really stepped in it with *that* generalization! I'm one of those 'people today,' and if we have such poor work ethics, why am I so darned tired at the end of each day? Look at the statistics and trends. With downsizing, flattening organizations, increased competition, and an ever-growing emphasis on 'doing more with less,' people in general are working longer and harder than ever before. I know *I* am!

"Granted, not everyone busts their buns around here. But that's not unique to today's workforce – it's characteristic of every time, every generation. **What 'people today'** *do* **have are greater expectations** for satisfying work, competent leadership, fair treatment and compensation, a stake in (and share of) the organization's success, and coworkers who carry their part of the load. Fail to make sure those are in place, and you'll miss out on the best that we 'people today' have to offer.

"When it comes to work ethics, do you yearn for 'the good old days'? Me, too! That's when most people worked only 40 hours a week. What a concept!

"Guess what? Now *I* feel better, too."

> *When people today complain about people today, aren't they complaining about themselves?*

39

if people don't meet expectations, send them to training

Sometimes this is right on target ... sometimes it's way off base (how's that for a mixed metaphor!). Think that training is the first and best response to **all** performance deficiencies? FORGET IT!

The first thing to do when people fail to meet expectations is to find out why. In other words, you have to *understand* the problem before you can select the appropriate solution to it.

If the problem is the result of a skill deficiency (i.e., the person doesn't know how), training may be the most effective response. Sometimes, however, problems come from a lack of information or from unclear expectations. In these cases, better communication is the likely solution. At other times, people may fail to meet expectations because of obstacles in the system that they just can't overcome by themselves. The solution here: Remove the obstacles ... or at least cut the folks some slack. Finally, some problems are attitudinal (i.e., the person knows what to do and how to do it but chooses not to deliver). Counseling and accountability are your best alternatives here – all the training in the world won't crack this nut.

So, forget training as a **universal** cure. We recommend you adopt this in its place:

> *If people don't meet expectations, find out why. Then choose a response that's appropriate for the situation ... one that makes common sense.*

> Beware of the doctor who prescribes surgery for a common cold.

Forget For Success
Order Form

82LL

$$\left.\begin{array}{r}1\text{-}99 - \$6.95 \text{ each}\\100\text{-}999 - \$6.45 \text{ each}\\1000\text{-}4999 - \$5.95 \text{ each}\\5000\text{-}9999 - \$5.45 \text{ each}\\10{,}000 \text{ or more} - \$4.95 \text{ each}\end{array}\right\}$$

Copies _____

Book Total $ _____

Shipping and Handling *(see chart below)* +$ _____

TOTAL $ _____

Texas Only – Sales Tax (8.25% of Total) +$ _____

TEXAS TOTAL $ _____

SHIPPING & HANDLING CHARGES:

Order $ Amount	Charges
Up to $50	$4
$50-99	$7
$100-249	$10
$250-649	$18
$650-1,299	$32
$1,300-1,999	$55
$2,000-3,499	$68
Over $3,500	Call

Outside the continental U.S., please call.

Orders shipped via UPS Ground. Next business day and second business day delivery is available. Please call for information.

☐ YES, please send me information on other WALK THE TALK® products and services to help turn organizational values into value-added results.

Name (MR/MS) _____

Title _____

Organization _____

Street Address _____

City, State, Zip, Country _____

Phone (   ) _____ Fax (   ) _____

Purchase Order Number (if applicable) _____

☐ MasterCard   ☐ VISA   ☐ AMERICAN EXPRESS Cards   ☐ Check Enclosed   ☐ Please Invoice
(Payable to: The WALK THE TALK Company)   (orders over $100 only)

Account Number _____ Exp. _____

Signature _____

Prices effective November 1997 are subject to change. Orders payable in U.S. dollars. Orders outside U.S. and Canada must be prepaid.

Three Ways To Order
Forget For Success

Call: 800.888.2811
Fax: 972.243.0815
Mail: The WALK THE TALK® Company
2925 LBJ Freeway, Suite 201
Dallas, Texas 75234-7614

(see order form on back)

Ask about our other high-impact publications:

- ***Walk The Talk ... And Get The Results You Want***

    The best-selling business book that shows leaders, at all levels, why and how to turn organizational values into value-added practices.

- ***144 Ways To Walk The Talk***

    The quick-reference handbook packed with proven ideas and strategies for practicing values-driven leadership.

- ***Walking The Talk Together: An Employee Handbook***

    The powerful handbook that encourages all employees to take responsibility for values-driven business practices.

- ***Walk Awhile In MY Shoes***

    The revolutionary *2-in-1* handbook that encourages understanding, empathy, and cooperation between managers and employees.

For information on these and other WALK THE TALK® products and services, call us at 800.888.2811 or visit our website at **www.walkthetalk.com**

WALK THE TALK

Values Based Business Solutions
The WALK THE TALK® Company
2925 LBJ Freeway, Suite 201, Dallas, Texas 75234-7614
972.243.8863 • Fax 972.243.0815 • www.walkthetalk.com

Important Words to FORGET

10 Words to Forget
It doesn't matter what I do – I'm only one person

9 Words to Forget
I'll change just as soon as everyone else does

8 Words to Forget
Do as I say, not as I do

7 Words to Forget
That's their opinion ... what do they know?

6 Words to Forget
Because I said so, that's why

5 Words to Forget
I win and you lose

4 Words to Forget
It's not my job

3 Words to Forget
I don't care

2 Words to Forget
Those people

1 Word to Forget
Me

Forgetting for Success

*T*he previous pages provide just a sampling of commonly held and accepted ideas, beliefs, and misconceptions that can be counterproductive to achieving the results you want – in both your professional and your personal life. Some of the topics probably struck a familiar chord ... others may have seemed totally irrelevant for you. Just know there's plenty more where these came from. To find them, all you have to do is look around, dig a little, and think a lot.

As we see it, the material addressed runs the gamut from ideas that seem to be acceptable at first glance, to those that are obviously problematic; from those that might have made sense at one time but don't serve us well now, to those that have never made sense at all. And some of the issues we've highlighted are not problems at all – we've just offered what we believe are more productive alternatives for your consideration.

Do we expect you to agree with everything presented? Of course not! As the old saying goes: "You can't please all of the people all of the time." Besides, total agreement wasn't our goal. What we've attempted to do is raise your awareness that all of us are susceptible to flawed beliefs and behaviors that ultimately shape the results we get and the relationships we experience.

To be sure, this book is not about "life or death" stuff. None of the beliefs or practices we've identified will result in your personal demise if left unchanged. But put enough of them together, and you'll end up with a critical mass that can diminish your effectiveness as an employee, a leader, and a person. That alone should be reason to pay attention.

So, how do you go about **forgetting for success?** You do it by examining individual beliefs and replacing them – as appropriate – with better, more effective ones. We offer the following checklist of questions as a guide:

- [ ] 1 What is a "people practice" that I and others frequently engage in?

- [ ] 2 What are the possible ways that practice might negatively impact people, performance, relationships, or results?

- [ ] 3 What is the belief or premise that underlies the practice?

- [ ] 4 How might that belief be modified to eliminate the negative impact and be more in sync with our organizational values?

- [ ] 5 What specific behavior(s) would be in sync with the modified belief?

- [ ] 6 What specifically can/will I do to adopt the new behavior(s) and belief?

- [ ] 7 What should I look for to determine whether or not the changes I've made have been effective?

Find the Hidden Message

```
N O I T I N G O C E R M D T
O C F R U L E S M H M A R S
S E E L P O E P T N A O G S
R L E A Y M A P G A P N T E
O E D A A T E N M P I F G N
I B B M H C I O U H E S A E
V R A Y C N R S C G U O M V
A A C A E M G A R A L L A I
H T K T N R O K E E A U M T
E E S R O C T N A T V T A C
B I A W M H A I A M D I M E
L E A D E R S H I P D O D F
L V A L U E S T E S A Ⓝ Ⓤ Ⓕ
T N E M T I M M O C A S E E
```

Three-word hidden message:

_____   _____   _____

Accept, Add Value, Behaviors, Celebrate, Change, Coaching, Commitment, Diversity, Effectiveness, Empathy, Feedback, **Fun**, Grow, Leadership, Learn, Listening, People, Recognition, Rules, Solutions, Support, Think, Values.

How To Play: (Read instructions completely BEFORE starting)

All the words listed above can be found in the puzzle – horizontally, vertically, diagonally, or backwards.

1. Find the words in the puzzle. <u>Circle the individual letters</u> of each word. DO NOT CIRCLE THE ENTIRE WORD in the puzzle.

2. As you find and circle the letters of each word in the puzzle, UNDERLINE the corresponding word in the word list. DO NOT CROSS OUT WORDS in the word list.

3. After you have found all the words in the puzzle, circle all remaining A's and M's.

4. The remaining uncircled letters make up a three-word hidden message. Write that message in the box above.

Highlights ...
to REMEMBER

- ❑ Rather than treating people equally, your goal should be to treat them *equitably*.

- ❑ Frequently notice and reinforce the kind of behavior and performance you want from others.

- ❑ In the long run, you'll be much better off using your best resources in areas of strength rather than problem zones.

- ❑ With few exceptions, different isn't wrong ... it's just different.

- ❑ You don't manage people, you *lead* them.

- ❑ The only time people know what you're thinking is when you *tell* them.

- ❑ It's not enough to just know your values. You need to *behave* them ... you need to walk the talk.

- ❑ One surefire way to succeed in business and life is to treat people the way *they* want to be treated.

- ❑ When dealing with performance problems, focus on problem solving and correction rather than punishment.

Continued

- ❏ See diversity for what it really is: a business success strategy.

- ❏ Look for and create opportunities to learn, grow, and continually improve.

- ❏ Encourage people to have fun, enjoy their work, and think.

- ❏ Lasting change doesn't come from doing a little a lot better. It comes from doing a lot a little better.

- ❏ The best developmental feedback is frequent, informal, and comes from multiple sources.

- ❏ Everyone is responsible for their own behavior.

- ❏ Empathy means walking awhile in someone else's shoes. It's about being considerate and understanding.

- ❏ Rules should be followed or changed, but not ignored.

- ❏ If people don't meet expectations, find out why. Then choose an appropriate response. Don't assume training is the answer.

Finally:

"I've got some ideas on what else to forget ... Unfortunately, they'll never get published"

*F*ORGET IT ... but don't forget *them* (your ideas).

We'd like to hear your thoughts – and perhaps publish them in our planned sequel: *Forget For Success II* or *More Stuff To Forget For Success* or *Forget For Success: The Next Generation* or some other yet-to-be-determined title.

Send us your ideas on what to forget – along with a one or two paragraph explanation for each – via:

Fax: Forget For Success Ideas
972.243.0815

OR

Internet: www.walkthetalk.com
(under *Forget For Success* book)

If your idea is selected, you'll get a byline credit and a special gift.

Hope to hear from you!

additional beliefs and practices to forget:

The WALK THE TALK® Company

*F*or over 20 years, the WALK THE TALK® Company has provided **V**alues-**B**ased **B**usiness **S**olutions for thousands of organizations worldwide, including General Electric, Amoco, Boeing, and PepsiCo. Your #1 source for turning organizational values into value-added results, we offer a full range of products and services – all designed to help build commitment, individual accountability, and productivity.

Our full range of WALK THE TALK resources includes handbooks, workshops, videos, assessment tools, and consulting services.

*The WALK THE TALK® Company Senior Management Team
(l-r) Kim Dickerson, Eric Harvey, Juli Baldwin,
James Johnson, Lauri Johnson, and Steve Ventura*

The Authors

*E*ric Harvey is an internationally known consultant, author, and speaker in the areas of values-based business practices and organizational change. With over 25 years of professional experience, he has authored seven acclaimed publications, including the best-selling *Walk The Talk ... And Get The Results You Want* – the forerunner to the popular WALK THE TALK® book series.

*S*teve Ventura is an award-winning writer and program designer, and has developed over 40 publications, training programs, and manuals. His background spans 20 plus years of human resources development experience in both private and public sectors.

Three Ways To Order

Call: 800.888.2811
Fax: 972.243.0815
Mail: The WALK THE TALK® Company
2925 LBJ Freeway, Suite 201
Dallas, Texas 75234-7614

(see order form on back)

Our high-impact publications:

- *Walk The Talk ... And Get The Results You Want*

    The best-selling business book that shows leaders, at all levels, why and how to turn organizational values into value-added practices.

- *144 Ways To Walk The Talk*

    The quick-reference handbook packed with proven ideas and strategies for practicing values-driven leadership.

- *Walking The Talk Together: An Employee Handbook*

    The powerful handbook that encourages all employees to take responsibility for values-driven business practices.

- *Walk Awhile In MY Shoes*

    The revolutionary *2-in-1* handbook that encourages understanding, empathy, and cooperation between managers and employees.

- *Forget For Success*

    The practical, easy-read that pinpoints counterproductive beliefs and people practices which negatively impact your culture and bottom line.

For information on these and other WALK THE TALK® products and services, call us at 800.888.2811 or visit our website at **www.walkthetalk.com**.

WALK THE TALK

Values Based Business Solutions

The WALK THE TALK® Company
2925 LBJ Freeway, Suite 201, Dallas, Texas 75234-7614
972.243.8863 • Fax 972.243.0815 • www.walkthetalk.com

Forget For Success
Order Form

1-99 – $6.95 each	
100-999 – $6.45 each	Copies _____
1000-4999 – $5.95 each	
5000-9999 – $5.45 each	Book Total $_____
10,000 or more – $4.95 each	

Shipping and Handling *(see chart below)* +$_____

TOTAL $_____

Texas Only – Sales Tax (8.25% of Total)+$_____

TEXAS TOTAL $_____

SHIPPING & HANDLING CHARGES:

Order $ Amount	Charges	
Up to $50	$4	*Outside the continental U.S., please call.*
$50-99	$7	
$100-249	$10	*Orders shipped via UPS Ground.*
$250-649	$18	*Next business day and second business*
$650-1,299	$32	*day delivery is available. Please call*
$1,300-1,999	$55	*for information.*
$2,000-3,499	$68	
Over $3,500	Call	

☐ YES, please send me information on other WALK THE TALK® products and services to help turn organizational values into value-added results.

Name (MR/MS)_____

Title_____

Organization_____

Street Address_____

City, State, Zip, Country_____

Phone (   )_____ Fax (   )_____

Purchase Order Number (if applicable) _____

☐ MasterCard   ☐ VISA   ☐ AMERICAN EXPRESS Cards   ☐ Check Enclosed   ☐ Please Invoice
(Payable to: The WALK THE TALK Company)   *(orders over $100 only)*

Account Number_____ Exp._____

Signature_____

Prices effective January 1998 are subject to change. Orders payable in U.S. dollars. Orders outside U.S. and Canada must be prepaid. Restocking fee charged for returned materials.